CHILDREN'S BIBLE CLASSICS

W9-BYK-383

THE STORY OF JONAH

Publishers Since 1798

THOMAS NELSON PUBLISHERS
Nashville

First published in 1993 by
Thomas Nelson Publishers, Nashville, Tennessee.

**Story retold by Bill Yenne
and Timothy Jacobs**

Edited by Lynne Piade. Art and design direction by Bill
Yenne. Illustrated by Pete Avdoulos, Mark Busacca, Emi
Fukawa, Victor Lee, Wendy K. Lee, Douglas Scott, Peggy
Smith, Alexandr Stolin, Vadim Vahrameev, Hanako
Wakiyama, Nelson Wang and Bill Yenne.

Produced by
Bluewood Books (A Division of The Siyeh Group, Inc.)
P.O. Box 460313, San Francisco, CA 94146

The Story of Jonah.
   p.   cm. — (Children's Bible Classics)
   Summary: A simple retelling of the Bible story in which
Jonah tries to resist the will of God and suffers the
consequences, on sea and on land.
   ISBN 0-8407-4915-5 (TR)
   ISBN 0-8407-4909-0 (MM)
   1. Jonah (Biblical prophet)—Juvenile literature.
2. Bible. O.T.—Biography—Juvenile literature.   3. Bible
stories, English—O.T. Jonah. [1. Jonah (Biblical prophet)
2. Bible Stories—O.T.]   I. Thomas Nelson Publishers.
II. Series.
BS580.J55S785   1993
224'.9209505—dc20   93-24837
                                                              CIP
                                                              AC

93 94 95 96 97—1 2 3 4 5

Printed and bound in the United States of America

THE
STORY OF JONAH

Once, long ago, there was a great city. It was called Nineveh and it was so big that it took a person three days to walk all the way around it. It was a large city, and the people who lived there were very mean and wicked.

God wanted someone to warn the people of Nineveh that He was not happy with the way they were living. He decided to send them a prophet. God chose Jonah to tell the people of Nineveh to repent.

Jonah was a very stubborn man. He did not want to preach to the people of Nineveh.

Because Jonah didn't want to do what God had asked, he ran away. He found a ship about to sail to Tarshish, a place far away to the west. He paid the fare and got on board.

Jonah should have known that he could not hide from God. God caused a great wind to blow across the water. Huge waves threatened to sink the ship.

Jonah was sound asleep, but the ship's captain woke him up. He told Jonah to ask God to make the storm stop.

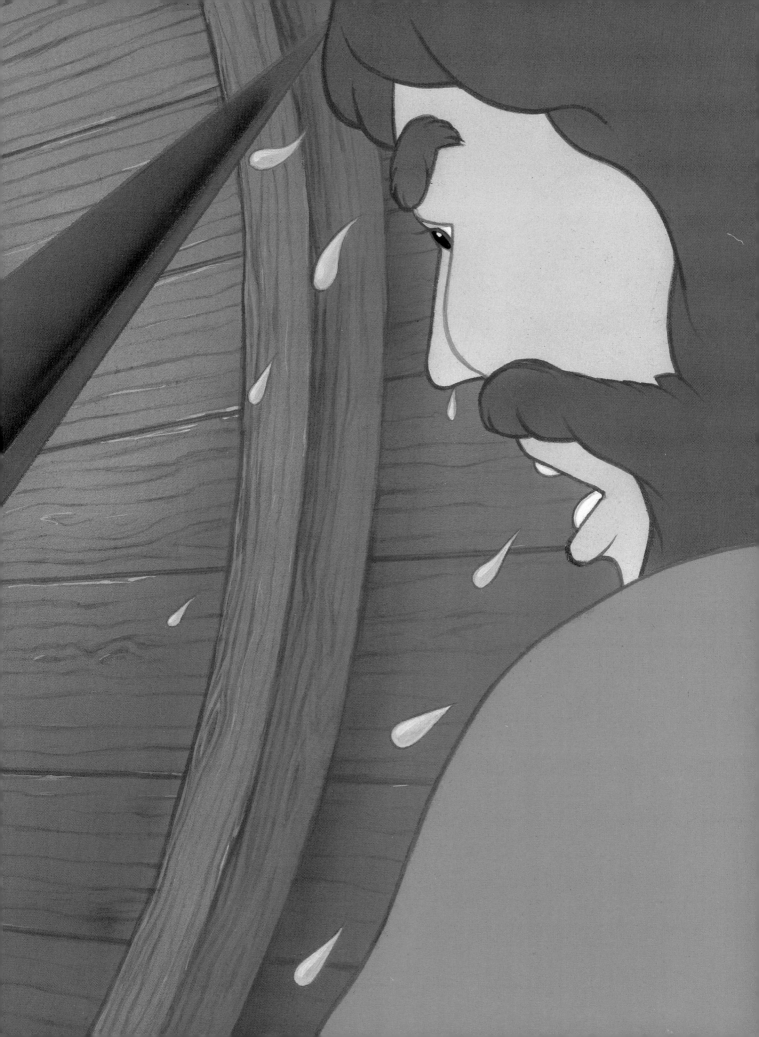

The sailors wanted to know why God was so angry. Why would God bring such a great storm? Jonah told the sailors how he had disobeyed God's orders to go to Nineveh. The sailors were afraid and mad at Jonah for putting them all in danger.

They tried to row the ship, but they couldn't. The sailors asked Jonah what they could do to make the storm stop. Jonah told them to throw him overboard.

They threw Jonah overboard into the sea. The storm stopped, and the water became calm.

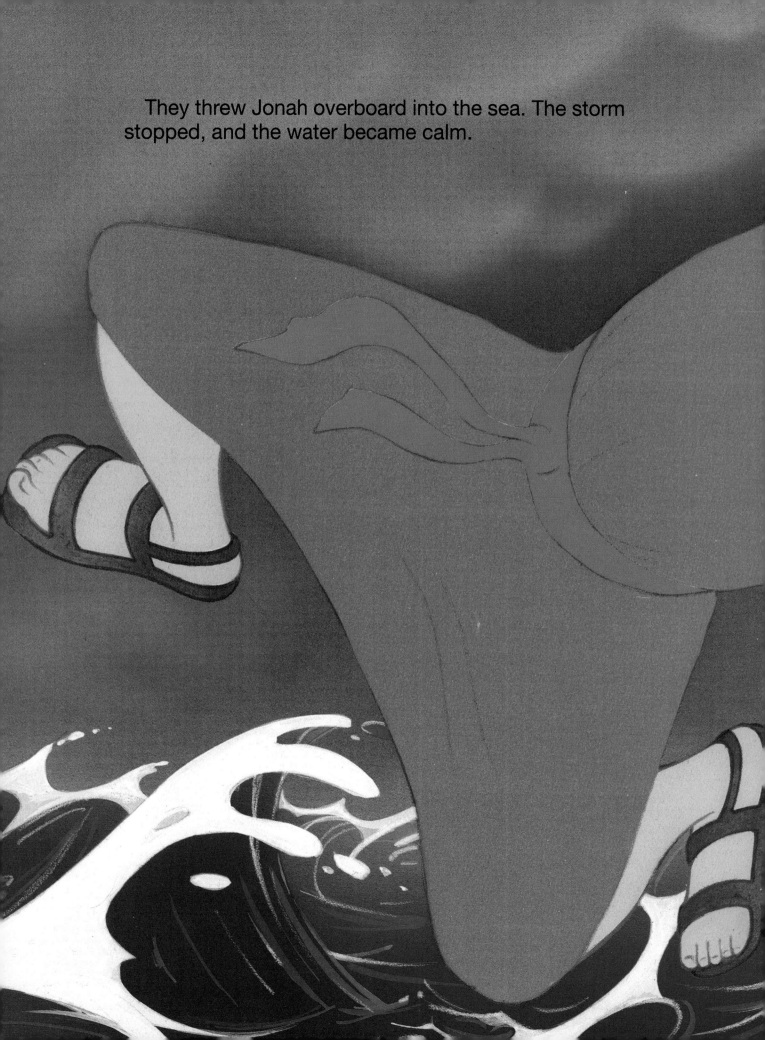

The Lord did not want Jonah to drown. When Jonah was thrown in the water, he was swallowed by a a gigantic fish!

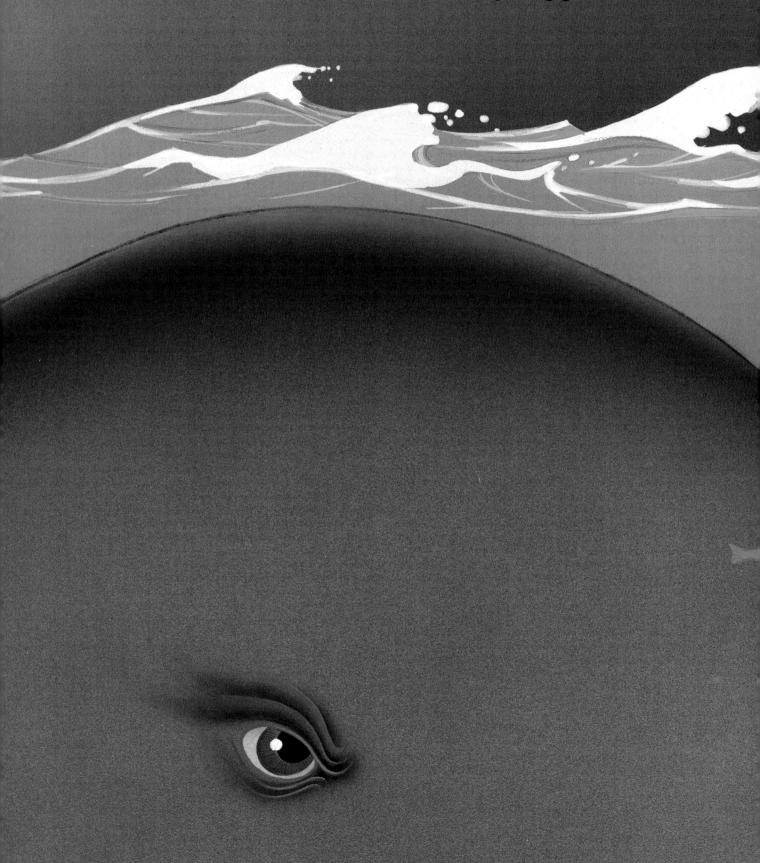

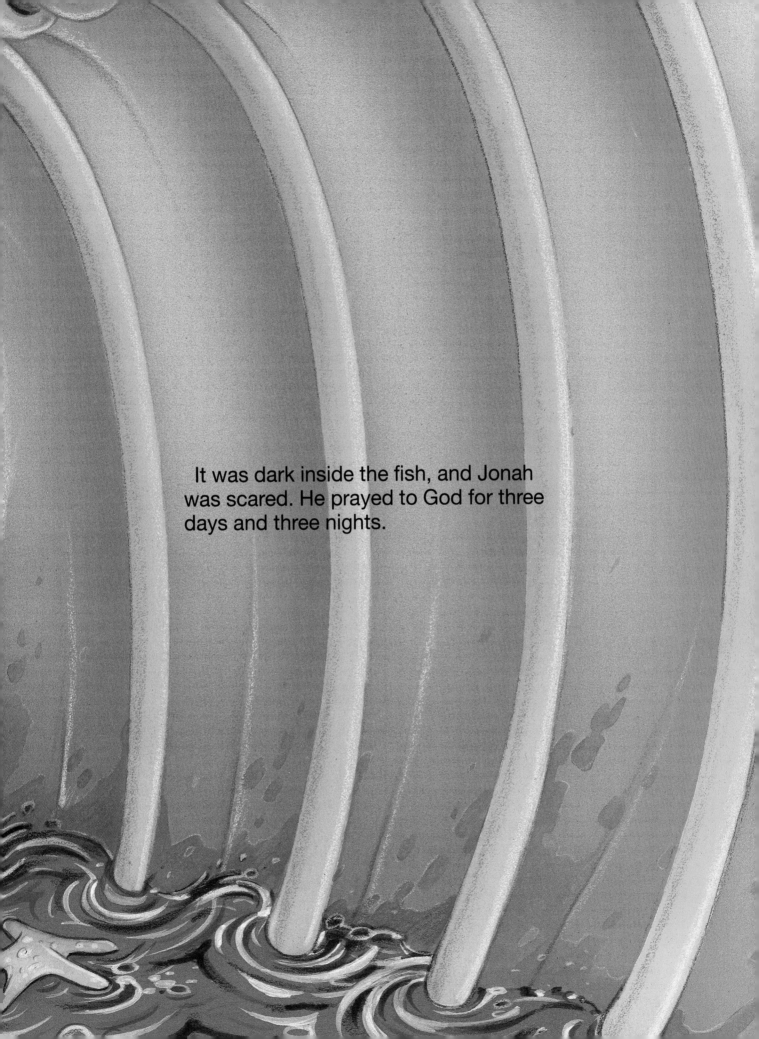

It was dark inside the fish, and Jonah was scared. He prayed to God for three days and three nights.

Then God told the fish to spit Jonah out on the coast near Nineveh.

God asked Jonah for the second time to go and warn the people of Nineveh that they must change their ways. This time Jonah obeyed God.

Jonah told the people that they had to live according to God's laws. If they didn't, God was going to destroy their city in forty days.

Jonah was doing what God said, but he wasn't happy.
He didn't like the people in Nineveh. But still he preached,
and the people of Nineveh believed Jonah.

Jonah was surprised. The people of Nineveh changed their ways and prayed to God.

Jonah was mad at God for forgiving the people of Nineveh and not punishing them. Jonah was very angry and miserable.

Jonah was a very stubborn man. He went into the mountains and camped on a spot where he could watch to see if God would change His mind and destroy Nineveh after all. The weather became very, very hot.

Even though Jonah was being stubborn, God felt sorry for him. God made a plant grow up and over where Jonah was sitting. The leaves gave Jonah a lot of shade.

Jonah was thankful for the plant, but that night while Jonah was asleep, God sent a worm to make the plant wither and die. The next day, the sun rose, the wind blew, and it was very, very hot. Jonah was so angry and hot he wished he were dead. But God was teaching Jonah an important lesson.

Jonah had not made the plant grow, but he was mad because it died. God said, "I gave the plant life, like I gave the people in Nineveh life. I care about what happens to them."

Jonah finally began to understand God's message. Jonah saw that he had been very selfish.

Jonah was happy for the first time in a long time. He learned that God loves and takes care of everyone who obeys Him.